STOP FIGHTING AND LET ME HEAL YOU

A CONVERSATION WITH GOD

Dr. Arlene Rose-Lewis

STOP FIGHTING AND LET ME HEAL YOU: A Conversation with God

ISBN : 978-976-96536-1-0

Book Cover Design : Sylvia M Dallas / Jason Johnson

Publisher : The Publisher's Notebook Limited

Email : **thepublishersnotebook@gmail.com**

Telephone: 876 331 0727

This book is dedicated

to the Lord God, for

it is by His love

that I live and breathe

Introduction

I was on a forty day fast one morning in the year 2020, seeking to hear from God regarding healing for other people, which is the thing that interests me most in this world.

On the morning of the 22nd day of the fast the words you are about to read began to flow out with an unstoppable force. I grabbed a pen and literally began to write by hand every word which is in this book. It took almost 10 hours to complete what was written in the voice of God as narrator. I wrote until my hands were sore. I have heard His gentle prompting before but never dreamed I would get a continuous ten-hour flow. The words spoke to me as I wrote, and I had personal moments of revelation as a sense of peace came over me.

To the best of my knowledge I am not unwell, but as a doctor I began to see things more clearly. I understood how to identify and overcome many of the roots of disease and what to do about them. It is my hope and expectation that for those of you who need to heal, you will begin to do so before you even finish reading this. It is also a kind of workbook, so I suggest you grab some paper or a notebook, because there are some healing exercises for you to do that will help you to derive as much benefit as you can from this. Many secrets of the soul-body connection will be revealed. This book is my gift to anyone who needs to heal now, once and for all, in body soul and spirit.

CHAPTER 1

I am your God. Many doubt My existence, but I am real and I love you and have always loved you. It was never My desire for anyone to be sick. You were meant to live among beauty and peace, with dominion and blessing: with animals, trees and abundant food and water.

When Adam ate the forbidden fruit, it gave the enemy of man access, and with it came all kinds of evil, including sickness. But I sent My Son to die as a perfect man without sin to take away the impact of all your sins, to take every disease, and every curse from you and your family.

If you can believe, all things will be possible for you. Your health will be restored. I will personally take you on a journey on which you will find that the secret to good health and a very blessed life was in plain view. It has always been. These secrets are among the pages of the Bible, which is a book that brings forth life. Every word is food for your soul.

Let's talk for a minute about your soul. It is meant to be a beautiful place where all your thoughts live, all your feelings abide. Once you were born, there began a series of hard moments of rejection, moments of shame, unworthiness and many evils. These were all ordained by the enemy of man.

You see My child, there is a book with your story in it. It is a story of overcoming. I have sent a special angel who is ever seated with me, and his agenda is to guide you, and to bless you exceedingly and abundantly more than you could ever imagine.

He is activated by your belief, by the words you speak, and by your faith. Can you stretch your faith? How far can it go? How much do you dare to believe? Do you believe that you can be healed? Can you believe this now? If you can believe then I will show you how, but first, I must congratulate you for picking up a book with this title, because something in your soul knew that you would be hearing My voice throughout these pages. Something in your soul needs to hear what I am about to say. Something in your soul craves to know Me.

I am here for you. I always will be, and always have been. Every challenge you have been through has been a teacher, a builder of strength, resilience and faith. Even though at times you have felt battered or broken by the enemy, I have been with you ensuring that you survived.

I will turn all things around for your good if you allow Me. It is written that what is in the heart defiles a man. I will now help you to heal your heart. I never force healing on anyone…it is a choice. You may treat sickness any way you choose, but there is always a root cause and if that is not addressed then you will only become sick again or simply not truly heal. I have seen so many of My children have surgery to cut a problem out, only to have it return, or the pain either remains or intensifies. I have seen so many medicaments being taken only to control the symptoms, **yet** these themselves weaken the body. This is not wisdom. Wisdom is removing the cause first.

My child, the cause often springs forth from the depths of the soul. In your soul there are unresolved, unsettled events and moments in time where it was injured by traumas, accusations, disappointments, and betrayals.

The time has come for these issues to be finally laid to rest. At times you may wrestle against yourself, and you may even cry tears of release, but your soul will be allowed to heal.

I have made the soul in such a way that the state of the soul controls the state of the body. Though you may have many scars that have healed in your flesh, your soul may have arrows, thorns, holes, bruises, and torn places, inflicted through the passage of time and interactions with others. Your perceptions of these events create the wounds.

In this world these will be trouble but behold I have overcome. Now it is time to see how to remove the enemy's access to your soul. Through the chapters of this book your soul will become healed, quickly followed by your body; and this is My deepest desire. May you prosper and be in health, even as your soul, your beautiful surviving soul prospers. Let us begin!

CHAPTER 2

*In the beginning was the word and the
word was with God... and the WORD
WAS GOD.... The word became flesh.*

My Son came to bring good news for you, and though this speaks of His coming I would like you to consider for a moment who you are.

You were made in My image. MY image. You were made to take domination over all living things. We will begin with dominion over your words and beliefs. Did you know that what comes out of your mouth can defile you? One of the greatest follies is to see My children speak loose words over their own lives.

They say things like "I'd rather die," or "I can't go on like this," or "I wish I could bear the pain for him/her." You must always remember that the enemy goes to and from in the earth waiting for you and others to speak such words, so that he can bring them to pass… he is a fallen angel. When My children say words like "I will live and not die" or "Thank you doctor for your recommendations, but only God knows when I will die and I will not be dying from this," My heart smiles as My holy angels rush out to bring life to them.

You see, when you speak the negative, life defeating words, you grant access to the enemy. You choose his way instead of Mine. Please remember you were made in My image. Your words take charge of your own life. Your words speak your choice. You choose whether you want to activate My holy angels or the enemy of your soul and body.

Here are some things which I have heard people say:

- "My father and grandfather and brothers died of this, so I guess it's only a matter of time."
- "I am pre-diabetic."
- "This food is to die for."
- "I would rather die."
- "I can't live another day with this."
- "My parents had it so I guess I will too."
- "Knowing how unlucky I am I'll probably get it."

There is an even greater folly which I must also make clear. You must also choose what you will believe. There are words spoken by parents or others in authority over children. If these words are received into the soul of the child, they form roots. Examples of these are:

- "You're worthless!"
- "you are a dish rag" or other such words.
- "you won't amount to anything"
- "you're not as good as ____________."
- "I wish you were never born."
- "you're no good at__________."
- "you are a sickly child."
- "you are a loser."

When I hear these words spoken over children, a great many things happen. The speaker releases negative effects over their own lives and if the child receives the words, they become a matter for overcoming and strength building later in the child's life. It becomes an area that once overcome, my children can help others on their journeys later on. If there is no experience in an area there is no authority in that area.

It has been set since the eating of the forbidden fruit that there would be trouble, but I have overcome it. I send people dreams, visions… I send help and support through My Holy Spirit so that you will overcome… and now, I have sent you this book.

Now, every word you have spoken against your life invites the enemy. Every negative word, and every thought you have believed invites him too.

Science too has even proven this over and over. There is one called Dr. Emoto, who proved the effect of words on water. I have made your body mostly of water, with a minor portion of dust. The water responds to every word… to every thought, even to every judgement you make of others. Every negative word you speak about another affects you the most and them to a lesser extent. I have made you like Myself. Now that you know the power that abides in your words, use them wisely. Words may make or break curses. Every negative defeating word which you or another has spoken over you can be broken right now… today. Every negative belief can be erased. I will teach you how to break the effects of all those words from your life. If you're ready, repeat these prayers out loud, see them come alive, and experience the feeling of freedom that comes when this part of your healing is complete.

"Heavenly Father, I thank You for giving my words power. I now repent of misusing that power against my own life and the lives of others. I repent of every negative word I have ever spoken. By Your Word Father, You have said that

through repentance You would be faithful to forgive me of all my sins. I now receive Your forgiveness, even as I forgive all who have sinned against me through their words against my wellbeing, success, health, life and purpose.

I forgive them completely, and now stand in my authority as a child of GOD and demand the enemy to cease all operations that have begun as a result of words spoken against me. Cease NOW! I break the power of the enemy now and command him to return sevenfold everything he has stolen from me or anyone I have spoken negatively about. I welcome and receive all my blessings now, Thank you Lord. Amen."

I am so proud of you! You should feel a weight lift from you. Exhale and just imagine the enemy removing the impact of every word curse from around your organs, joints, teeth and even your brain, mind and heart. Your soul is healing in a few vital areas right now. A measure of health and blessings that was meant for you and waiting for you, is now going to have access to you because of this work. There is one more thing I'd like you to do, and this will be deeply personal. These are some words you have heard that need to be replaced. They were so unfair to you, but today is the day that they will be replaced by new words. Let Me give you an example. A doctor told one of My children that he would be paralyzed, never walk again and never get to play his beloved cello again. He cancelled that word and told the doctor that he would not only play but perform on a grand stage within three months. I can tell you I was so delighted as My angels set out to assist him, while the enemy sat, paralyzed by his words.

So now let's exchange a few of your most hurtful ones. Write them down here. What words spoken over you have hurt the most.

1. _______________________________________

2. _______________________________________

3. _______________________________________

4. _______________________________________

5. _______________________________________

6. _______________________________________

7. _______________________________________

8. _______________________________________

9. _______________________________________

10. ______________________________________

11. ______________________________________

12. ______________________________________

And now they have lost power. What better words will you replace them with! Please, give the holy ones a task of blessing in your life to replace each of those hurtful dead words with life giving words of blessing.

Be creative, speak the new words over yourself to cancel and replace the old ones. Write them down in the space provided below. Let those old words dry up now and themselves die. May these new statements anchor into your soul and become your new reality as you write them. Here is an example. "I am able to do all things through Christ who strengthens me." For more examples, you may refer to the 'Healing scriptures' section at the back of this book, although they don't have to be from the Bible. They should however be strong enough to cancel the painful words that you have listed above.

New replacement (blessing) statements.

1. ____

2. ____

3. ____

4. ____

5. ____

6. ____

7. ____

8. _______________________________

9. _______________________________

10. ______________________________

11. ______________________________

12. ______________________________

Great job my beloved. You should repeat these new replacement words over yourself as often as is needed, to stamp the former words out of your mind. Now we are ready to move on to the next chapter of your healing journey.

CHAPTER 3

I watched as one of My daughters heard the news of her sister's suicide. She was in a state of numbness for several weeks. Her sister had chosen death insistently although I had brought her back from the brink many times. This was her absolute choice. Now I watched as My daughter wept. Her parents, themselves trying to cope had blamed her for the suicide.

The enemy is indeed an accuser of saints. She became angered but tried to cover it up and just move along. The sun set and rose many days over her anger which was buried deeply under a mask of being 'fine'. The words "I'm fine" do not heal deep anger, disappointment, betrayal, or sadness very well. They are like a scab under which all manner of infected material live. This poisons the soul and the body as well.

Before long, her heart began to surround itself with water in an attempt to protect itself. The valves began to weaken. Trying to suppress your feelings is like trying to keep a beach ball full of air under water. A great deal of energy needs to go into that act, and this steals the energy and resources that are needed to sustain health. Sadly, her heart began to break as her soul was broken. The ball cannot remain hidden. It always surfaces, and often manifests as sickness.

She did what the world does, got the diagnosis and lots of tests, all of which came back negative, cause unknown, but the problems were still there…the roots were still wrapped around her heart.

She tried natural remedies, ones that I Myself made, which are excellent remedies that would have worked, but for the root of the sickness.

Over time with no change in her scans she finally turned to Me, for My way. She was led to forgive her sister, to forgive and release her parents and to forgive herself. At this moment, the enemy let go. He had no choice but to remove the roots of sickness. The disease ceased to progress.

In a moment of meditation and seeking Me, My Son Jesus went to her in a vision and delivered a new heart for her. This was confirmed by the doctors. Her heart no longer needed to protect itself with fluid because she was now allowing divine protection. All the damaged valves healed. Angels had ministered to her and this great tribulation became a great lesson in overcoming… a lesson which exposes to others that it's not impossible to remove the roots of any disease if you'll just stop fighting and let Me heal you.

Here are some roots of disease. You will need to search yourself honestly, and admit which ones live below your scars. Which ones are in the beach ball that you have been fighting to keep hidden?

I must caution you, it is ok to experience fear for a moment, because it can protect your life. However, if it overcomes you and 'lives' within you, it becomes a root that can easily steal your health. Fear can change a mild brush with illness into a life threatening one. If prolonged it may also invite the enemy to cause that which you fear to occur, and I have not given you that spirit.

Likewise, with anger, which is a natural response to a hurt or an injustice. Do not let the anger become your constant companion. My word warns you not to let the sun go down on your anger. Forgive quickly and move on. Look for the lessons, the strength, and your story of overcoming.

Grief is a thing that is necessary, however if it becomes a thing that paralyses your life for a very long time, it becomes a root for sickness. Often the root of prolonged paralyzing grief abides in the chest area or bowels. I have had children who can't release their loved ones from their souls, and this manifested as constipation, or uncontrolled weight gain, chronic coughs, or even asthma.

My children, dwelling on all these negative emotions will not serve you. In My word it is written.

> *"Whatever things are true, whatsoever things are honest, whatsoever things are just, whatsoever things are pure, whatsoever things are lovely, whatsoever things are of good report, if there be any virtue and if there be any praise, think on these things."*

Right there, hidden in plain view in Philippians 4 is the recipe for good health peace of mind. It is My peace which is available. Peace, hope, joy, unconditional love, and the fulfillment of your purpose is what brings your body in line with the good health that I have promised to you. Sickness simply cannot live in this kind of environment, which we must now create within your soul so that your body can heal.

The first step is through forgiveness. Many of My children ask Me how they can truly forgive...even seemingly unforgivable things. There are some things that can only be forgiven with My help. Many insist that they can forgive, but they won't forget. Children, it is My desire to *FORGET* your sins. As you repent and live a life that is according to My plans for you, I will *remember your sins no more*, as it is written in Hebrews 8:12. No matter what you did, and I know everything about you, nothing can separate you from My love. So now, for your own health and wellbeing, it's your time to forgive. Let Me teach you how to say a prayer of forgiveness, so that you can be free. I know that there are many for you to forgive. Be honest with yourself now…nothing is hidden from Me.

List the names of the persons you need to forgive and please include your own name. Begin at the moment of your birth until the present.

1. _______________________________________

2. _______________________________________

3. _______________________________________

4. _______________________________________

5. _______________________________________

6. _______________________________________

7. _______________________________________

8. _______________________________________

9. _______________________________________

Very good job! There are yet more but these will be the major ones and forgiving them will bring you much freedom.

A son of mine had a severe bowel disease. He yet lives and is a medical specialist at the highest levels of his profession. Nothing he tried would help him to recover, and he was in this place of trying for over ten years. I sent him a bringer of truth and he began what the world calls 'Forgiveness' therapy. He found peace, removed the root and became well again after much chasing after the wind.

A daughter of mine was very angry with her former husband. No doctor could help her when sickness after sickness attached themselves to her. She began to take many medicaments, prescribed by many doctors. Diabetes, hypertension, and finally the legs refused to walk without the assistance of a stick to support her body. She was not at that age when walkers and sticks might become necessary. I sent a visionary into her path and the truth was revealed about the need for forgiveness. Quickly she forgave him and let go of the anger, as the roots of her disease were uprooted one by one. Within two months there was no trace of diabetes or hypertension, and no need for the walking stick.

I must tell you that what we are after is total forgiveness. No roots of bitterness must be left. Leave the forgetting to Me. I will remove the pain from the memories. There are some who have hurt you that require your prayers more than your presence at this time, because they have yet to receive and accept My truth. Your job is to overcome, and to do it as soon as possible. This will enable you to grow and truly shine, as you reflect My peace and wellbeing more and more.

I will now lead you in a prayer of forgiveness for others. You make the decision, and I will remove the pain and sickness caused by your unforgiveness. Let us begin as you speak these words out aloud. Please substitute the word 'her' whenever you are forgiving a female and do them one at a time as I remove each root.

"Heavenly Father, I am sorry for my sins against others, myself and You. I am sorry for all the persons who have been hurt by my actions. I know with my repentance You are willing to forgive me and cleanse me and FORGET my sins. I now, by Your example choose to release (insert name) for all the sins he has committed against me. In particular, the sins of (insert sins).

I forgive him completely, so that on judgement day, I will not point a finger at him. He is set free today from my judgement. He is free and I am now free." (Now let's pause for a moment to exhale all that hurt and inhale your freedom as we continue).

I now release a blessing for him into every area of his life, even as I now become able to receive Your blessings. I now welcome and receive every single blessing that has been held back from me resulting from unforgiveness. I receive restoration particularly in my health. Thank you, Lord!

Amen."

Now if you completed that prayer for one person you can do it for all of them. Take your time and do this for the persons who hurt you the most first. You will feel the shift in your soul and body. I will be here unravelling and uprooting the impact of sickness from your body, which I have created with great pride, before the enemy arrived. I will replace broken parts and seal all wounds, repair damaged areas as you reclaim your soul and body, piece by piece. I will remove every thorn, every arrow and every spear, all inflammation, every abnormal growth, and every infection from you. The more peace you receive in your soul, the more access to My healing you allow. Take a moment now and complete that prayer for everyone on the list that you have made.

******

Now it's time to forgive *yourself*. Speak the following words out aloud and really mean them. It's OK to truly deeply forgive yourself.

"Father, as I forgive my fellow man, I repent of all my sins. I know that you are faithful to forgive them and now I choose to forgive myself for everything I've ever done that was not pleasing to You. I release myself completely even as I become aware that You have already forgiven me. I let myself off the hook, even as You erase my sins from Your book and FORGET them. I choose to FORGET my own sins also and turn away from them now. I choose to free myself from self-condemnation. I know I fall short of perfection, so I choose to receive Your help as I go through the rest of my life. I now receive all the blessings that the enemy has been keeping from me because I had not forgiven myself. I receive total freedom, health and wholeness. Thank You my Lord. Amen."

21

And now I am certain that you are feeling lighter, freer even.

Many roots are now being uprooted. With each prayer more of My glorious light pours into your soul. How precious is the taste of freedom? Bask in it for a moment. Enjoy it. Feel the lightness in your body. Do not be surprised if through these exercises, you cry, or even cough because as you are being freed there may be physical manifestations of release.

You are doing so well. If you have completed these exercises you are now ready for the next chapter of your journey.

CHAPTER 4

In the former chapter I mentioned the impact of harboring emotions that are akin to expending daily energy to keep a beach ball underneath the water. We are now going to bring the ball gently to the surface and let the air out so that you will be able to spend your energy on being you, and on living the life which you were meant to live. It is prudent to do this before we delve into the purpose for your life.

Take a moment now to examine how you have been feeling over the past years or months, for the entire period of your sickness. Let's look back at when you first found out you were sick. What was happening just before then, how did you feel? Were you stressed, worried, pressured, lost, hopeless, scorned, betrayed, feeling like you didn't belong, feeling worthless or numb? Were you cast aside, overworked, too self-driven, condemned, accused, mistreated, grieving, lonely, judgmental, anxious, fearful, or guilty, or facing an unfair situation? Let us take a look at these in Table 1.

<u>Table. 1. What stole your peace?</u>

Anger	Condemnation of self
Fear	Condemnation of others
Worry	Prolonged grief
Anxiety	Excessive responsibility for others
Feeling unloved	Loneliness/depression
Rejection	Guilt
Abandonment	Poverty
Lack of belonging	Strife (with others)
Worthlessness	Trauma
Failure to progress	Torment
Ignored	Abuse
Shame	Self-pity
Too much self-drive	Excess need for attention
Violence	Hatred
Malice	Desire for vengeance
Jealousy	Greed
Fear	Judgement of self/others
	Hopelessness
	Despair

List any that applies to you:

1. ____________________________________

2. ____________________________________

3. ____________________________________

4. ____________________________________

5. ____________________________________

6. ____________________________________

7. ____________________________________

8. ____________________________________

9. ____________________________________

10. ___________________________________

11. ___________________________________

12. ___________________________________

By now some of these factors may be losing their grip on you simply by virtue of being exposed.

Any stressful events that occurred before your diagnosis give clues to the elements that need to be replaced. Sometimes it's difficult to admit your true feelings but the truth will free you. I will see to it.

Now if there are any other persons who have not yet been forgiven that have surfaced in your mind, forgive them now. Just go back, forgive them, and meet Me back right here.

Now we have forgiven all involved parties, and identified the feelings left behind from the events leading up to the sickness. Let us now evict each health-stealing emotion by calling their names, releasing them, and replacing them. Here is a list of just a few of the replacements that are available to you. Have a look at them, and then we will proceed to a prayer to replace the hurtful unwanted 'thieves of your peace' with My 'health restoring' gifts for you.

<u>Table 2   Health restoring gifts</u>

Strength	Favor
Unconditional love	Health
Gentleness to self	Prosperity
Freedom	Abundance
Peace	Hope
Joy	Purpose
Success	Self-worth
Acceptance of others	Adoption
Companionship	Belonging
Blessings	Self-acceptance

I will show you how to pray with one example that you can adapt. This may seem simple, but it is powerful.

Repeat after Me but substitute the appropriate emotion from your list. For now, I will demonstrate using anger.

"<u>Anger</u>, you have spent too much time in my soul. It's now time to end our relationship. I am now letting go and sending you away. You must now leave my body, soul and spirit because you never should have been here, especially not for this long. I command you to leave me now and take all your work against me.

<u>Anger,</u> I now replace you with, <u>peace, joy, freedom, hope, health, (or other replacement emotion)</u>. I am free, and your space is now occupied. You, <u>anger,</u> are forbidden to return to me by the GRACE, POWER and MERCY of God. Thank You, Lord for <u>(replacement).</u>

(You can new exhale and activate your faith by 'seeing' it through your eyes of your mind, slip away from you as it leaves your environment, home, and country taking with it all its actions against you).

As you do this exercise for all the chosen emotions and feelings, you will really be tapping into deeper levels of peace. Please take the time to do this for yourself, because this is *very* important. As you say the prayer above, you may replace torment with My gifts that will restore your peace and freedom. Consider it the recovery of ground or land space that has been occupied by unwanted squatters, and their replacement by new blessings in your life. This is exactly what will be happening, so take your time and do not rush this part. Experience each exchange as you speak the words. Once you complete this exercise it will be time to move on.

This replacement exercise is powerful, but it is going to take a little time if you really listen deeply and are honest. As we go along you are improving your ability to hear My voice. I will also guide you to know what other changes to your lifestyle can help you. You will be able to cut through the noise and get to the truth of what will help.

You are doing well…and now it's time to proceed to the next chapter of your healing.

CHAPTER 5

I will now delve into the essence of who you are and why you are on planet Earth. Many are of the misguided notion that they are here to get all they can get from others. This is a set up for dissatisfaction and disappointment. There are some things that are destined to be yours, and some things that are not. Favor and blessings and even abundance is designed for you… but if they become the major focus of your life, you have stepped off the path and are subject to the enemy's folly.

Some are of the notion that they are here to save everyone and prove their value in the process. They are many shepherds among you, many leaders who will indeed help others in mighty ways, but if it becomes the only thing in life at the expense of everything else, then it becomes an idol. This behavior may lead to a desperate seeking of affirmation, a need which can never be fully satisfied, because your value and worth comes from the fact that you are made wonderfully by Me. Relentless striving at the expense of your own health makes no sense. You were crafted with pride as I sang over you and saw that you were indeed VERY GOOD. My children must recognize situations in which they are to allow Me to do My work. So many sicken themselves trying to change a husband, a wife, a parent, or even an adult child. This is great folly. Why not do what you can and are supposed to do, and let Me do the rest? I love your loved ones more that you do. You are in total control of only your happiness.

There are boundary lines available to all humans, they are lying in a heap waiting to be utilized and secured in place. These boundaries are drawn not through prayer, but through conversations between yourself and others. This is about identifying that which is being allowed to control your life and, putting a stop to it.

Anyone, or anything that controls you is an idol. Whether it is a husband who you're allowing to beat you repeatedly, a parent, employer, child or sibling whom you are allowing to manipulate you, control you with force, or belittle you, this is not My will for you. If you feel excessively controlled, or fearful of stepping outside the will of another human being, then this becomes a matter which is stealing your peace. Now recall I said that health is welcomed and nurtured by peace of mind.

This can be a challenging matter because there is a false guilt that will often be experienced when you retake control of your own life and lay a boundary. This false guilt is a lie, so call it by its name (False Guilt) and send it away with its suitcase just like you did all the other negative peace-thieves. Replace it, and it will have to go.

There is often some kind of lie that has kept you stuck. You must identify it and find the truth. Here are some examples of such lies.

- *"I can't survive on my own without _______.*
- *"If I let go, _______ will die."*
- *"_____________ can't handle the truth."*
- *"If only I could do better, then _____________ would be happy."*
- *"I am the only person ______ speaks to, so I have to listen to all his/her woes."*
- *"It's too late for me now."*
- *"I have to put up with this because it's the right thing to do."*
- *"I have no choice!"*

Please look deeply for the truth. It is not My will for My children to suffer. If you are suffering at the control of another, you have shifted outside of My will.

There are some seemingly impossible situations, where you may feel stuck and there seems not to be any correct way to lay a boundary.

I see several of My children with who are caring for a parent at great cost to themselves, and though they have siblings, no one else is willing or able to help share the responsibility. This is an example of a case where My children can feel 'stuck' leading to sickness.

I must acknowledge that those who take responsibility, truly honor their parents and will be entitled to long life if they can avoid anger and bitterness because of the inactivity of their siblings. Step one is to forgive the siblings, especially if they can help but won't. Step two would be to check in with your purpose and let Me show you the solution. I am God, and I can make a stream appear even in the desert. I can create solutions, enlist solutions and activate and send help from unfathomable sources. Seek My will in every situation and I will be faithful to you. When I do send solutions, though, please do not let the lie stand between yourself and the help you need, especially if you are unwell. Do not be afraid to have the difficult conversations and lay the necessary boundaries you will need to get well.

When you are too close and can't see the solution, allow your mind to back up for a moment. Take some time away from the situation to check in with your purpose, and then allow me to work. This is also written in plain view in the Bible. *"All things work together for good for those who love God, and to them who are called according to his purpose"* (Romans 8:28)

Now let's return to purpose. Why are you on this Earth? Look at your fingertips, every fingerprint uniquely created, every organ in your body was made to support your life in some way. The three reasons for your life are:

1. to bless others with what I have put inside you,
2. to enjoy your calling and purpose
3. to bring about My will on the Earth.

Quite simply, you are here to love your neighbor, love yourself in humility, and to love your God.

Allow Me to explain further. Each one of you has unique talents. Your experiences will be added to those talents to create a stronger and more resilient you, enabling you to be an even greater blessing to the World.

Your story, everyone's story is meant to be a story of overcoming and blessing others. Each of My children is uniquely drawn to a talent or skill. All are good at something. I made it such that each would deeply enjoy the performance and use of that skill. Some have many skills, but as they learn to listen to My voice, everything connects, as the big picture becomes clear. Everything unfolds as you seek Me in the still moments.

The deepest call of your heart may be masked by the voices of others who are being used by the enemy of man to derail you. You may have been told you were no good at that which is to be your destiny. You then must find your way back to it as you answer the call of your heart.

There are many scientists who are employed as bankers, teachers, accountants, and also many artists and creative persons sitting behind desks doing unrelated tasks. This represents a chasing after the wind and will numb your soul. It drains the joy of living and attracts sickness like nothing else.

Purpose is the number one bringer of joy and is food for your soul. Purpose needs to be nurtured and attended to in some way, even though the manifestations of it may change with the seasons of your life.

I'll give you an example. An older woman who loves dancing and has danced professionally since age nine, finds she can no longer dance because of an injury. She may now teach it to others to continue her involvement with her purpose, or she may simply watch dancers dance and recall the days fondly with other retired dancers. She may, depending on how advanced in years she is, switch to the new purpose of enjoying her grandchildren, or assisting with the dance troupe at her church.

There is always a way to nurture and keep your purpose alive, no matter what the limitation. Your task is to discover it, dust it off, and 'feed' it regularly.

When purpose is gone, hope and joy give way to an endless numb existence. This is not My plan for you. Why not make a list right now of some of your strengths, gifts and talents. (Examples: interacting with people, creative, administrative, farming, supporting, teaching, healing, dance, writing, etc.)

1. ___________________________________

2. ___________________________________

3. ___________________________________

4. ___________________________________

5. ___________________________________

6. ___________________________________

7. ___________________________________

Which two of these are the most enjoyable? Circle them. It really is time to start enjoying your gifts now, no matter what else you find yourself doing to make ends meet. I will lead you into the fullness of purpose in due time. There is no pressure, just keep seeking My guidance, and being open. Your purpose will find you.

One of My older children with cancer made regular trips to an undertaker to plan for her death. This can hasten and invite death. I would like you now to make plans for life as though there were no limitations. With Me all things are possible. Whatever you are going through now will not last forever. Let's invite the good times so that I can send the angels out to make them happen for you. Don't believe Me? Try it. If it is in line with your purpose and will bless you, just write it down. What would you love to be doing? Now fill in the blanks for yourself.   Let's go!

1. ___________________________________

2. ___________________________________

3. ___________________________________

4. ___________________________________

5. ___________________________________

6. ___________________________________

7. ___________________________________

Excellent job. You just did the equivalent of *writing down your vision and making it plain on stone tablets, that he may run who reads it.* Write it, because writing is very powerful and it will bless you to read the words often. I will release angels to get you onto that path. You will then have to choose to take the first step.

This will restore a sense of hope and enjoyment to your life because this breeds good health. Once you have written your vision, try to look at it every day for many days. You will then be able to see opportunities as I cause their release into your life and get you ready for your journey.

I have had many children who have recovered from even stage 4 cancers by committing to self-care and authenticity. It is not a selfish thing to love oneself. In fact,

"*Love thy neighbor as thyself*," makes it clear that you must love yourself first before you can love others as much as yourself. This is not sin unless you love only yourself.

Healthy self-love is not selfishness, it is a necessity. It is *not* born out of listening to what others say about you, it should be because of a belief and security in understanding who you are, and what special things I have put inside you.

Self-love will protect you from prolonged abuse and enable you to take your feelings seriously enough to move away from an environment that doesn't serve you, or from persons who continually vex your spirit. It should even allow you to do things that feed your spirit and spend more time with people who support you and your purpose.

Let's take a moment of stock-taking to evaluate the things and persons that nurture and support you and the things and persons that drain you.

Who nurtures and supports your healing and/or purpose? List the names here.

Which persons do *not* support your healing and/or purpose?

____

____

____

____

____

What aspects of your environment support you?

____

____

____

____

____

What aspects of your environment do *not* support you?

____

____

____

____

____

Please be sure to harbor only unconditional love and understanding as you delicately put space between yourself and those who do not support you in the areas of health and purpose. These persons who do not support you are at different stages and are often themselves going through a lot. Be gentle with their souls, but be deliberate because you are now creating the environment needed for you to heal!

What could you do to create a more nurturing, wholesome environment? Consider even your home and lifestyle. Are there many old dead items that need to be removed? What can you add to your environment to bring more joy and life to it? What can you spend more time doing? Writing your answer here is a commitment to doing them. I will help you!

1. ________________________________

2. ________________________________

3. ________________________________

4. ________________________________

5. ________________________________

Now we are really moving. Please make a step by step timeline to surround yourself with more support as much as you can. An excitement should be returning to you now. Some things you will be able to change and some things you may not be able to change. Start with what you can change and leave the rest to Me. I will create the opportunities for you. It is My greatest desire to heal you and I have already begun.

There is one more thing of grave importance that I must bring to your attention. I am a God who detests cursed objects and objects used in the worship of other gods.

There are objects made by certain humans with the intention of harming the owners. They really do exist. Please look around you for any work of art, statue, or relic that you may have acquired that brings an uneasiness to your spirit, including relics used in the worship of other gods. If you choose to keep these by your free will, it can be an invitation for the enemy to spoil an area of your life. So many of My children step into a season of blessing when they get these objects out of their homes and separate themselves from idols and occult objects. It may be as simple as a T-shirt with skulls on it, or even a scarf, or tapestry. It may be a figurine with an animal head on it, or a decorative sword or even a piece of jewelry. Be very careful what you invite into your environment! If this is outside your current belief system, test it. Remove the suspicious objects from your home and see how your life improves, often within the first two weeks.

Many believe the rules I created were to limit their lives, but the truth is that they are to protect people from the enemy, deny his access to killing their bodies, stealing their blessings and destroying their lives. By following the guidelines outlined in My word, you make your own life more blessed and protect yourself from many afflictions.

Let's move on now to one of the most important aspects of your healing.

CHAPTER 6

One of my children had cancer of the reproductive system. She was very concerned and wanted to be healed as soon as possible. The doctors worked on her, but her symptoms seemed stubborn. With every flare in her condition her daughter would fly in from overseas to be with her. How she relished the closeness, attention, and quality time she spent with her. How her church sisters prayed, until one made the tentative suggestion, that perhaps she was afraid of losing the closeness with her daughter if she were well, and perhaps that was blocking her recovery. She sat appalled as the truth went to work at setting her free.

Deep within your heart, you will have to utterly want the sickness gone from you or it will simply not go. If you get attention, care and love because of it and you enjoy that, the enemy will be only too happy to allow it to progress causing you to die before the appointed time. I urge you to find another way to get the quality time and affection.

Another one of My beloved children who no longer walks the Earth, fell 'asleep' before his appointed time. He was the center of attention with his friends as he spoke at length about his suffering, showing photographs of the fluid that was removed previously collected in his abdomen from the cancer. He did not need to die, but he loved the 'benefits' of the disease and the enemy took advantage of that fact. This was a sad thing for his family, although he will inherit salvation.

I have mentioned that what is in the heart defiles a man. Please make sure that every part of your soul and spirit are in agreement that the disease that your doctors have diagnosed is going away. It must be utterly rejected by your soul and body.

Why not speak these words out aloud?

"Sickness, not this body! Not today, not ever! You are of no value to me and I command you to leave now. I have received clarity regarding what is needed to change in my life, so that it will support my health more and more each day. Your time is up. I send you away. May every root cause be uprooted now by the power of God and based on the finished work of Jesus Christ on the cross.

I come out of agreement with every diagnosis of sickness and with every prognosis proclaimed over me. I reject them as I choose to receive my complete healing now. Enemy, take all your work and leave now, slip out of my body, my pores, my feet, by whatever means you will leave completely. There is no aspect of sickness that I welcome and every ounce of it leaves now. It ends here and now! In place of sickness, I receive peace, hope, joy, unconditional love for myself and others, as well as healing of my body soul and spirit. I step into my authority as God's child and claim my healing now."

I command my body to renew and repair itself now. All inflammation and infection, every toxin and abnormal growth, every imbalance, malfunction and blockage leave now! Dry up now and disintegrate by the fire of God. No remnant of this sickness is allowed to remain!

I will not die but LIVE. I will fulfill my purpose. I will be a blessing to others in this world. Every symptom of this disease must leave my body now. By this time tomorrow I will feel better and with every passing day I will feel better and better until I am well. This is how it shall be by the Grace of God.

For every diseased organ, I receive a new healthy one right now from the store houses of heaven, hand-picked for me by my Father. Thank You Lord.   Amen!"

I am doing it now. It is happening. Can you feel it? Please feel free to say this prayer daily and then try to do more and more things that you couldn't do. Daily, train yourself to sense the shifts that are occurring in your body.

"If anyone says to this mountain,
go, throw yourself into the sea and does
not doubt in their heart but believes that
what they say will happen, it will be done
for them. (Mark 11:23)

My Son said this, and He meant it. Develop and grow your faith. Choose to believe. As you believe, please do not put toxic things into your body, and do not harbor toxic complaining or blaming thoughts into your mind.

Recovery can be immediate, but for some it will be a daily walk. Your speed of recovery will be determined by how quickly you can get back in line with peace, hope, joy and your purpose.

Some of My children have done everything they ever wanted to do and were ready to go from this life. Saints prayed for life, but My children were ready to move on. The heart's desire of the person who is ready to go, will often over-rule all other yearnings and prayers. It is written that I set before you life and death, so choose life. Choose life My child, until it is your appointed time. Life brings opportunities and many blessings.

Keep your thoughts from complaining. With every thought you either feed sickness or destroy it. Take them captive. Let them be as positive as you can make them. Stay away from blaming others. Choose what you will do as a result of the actions of others, without getting lost in questions like, "why" or "how could he or she?" Recognize the heart behind critical words or hurtful deeds. Is there truth hidden there that can benefit you? Can you make a change that will make you better? If not, then forgive quickly and move right along, refusing to be shaken from your sense of self-worth or purpose. Be grateful for the lessons, and if there are none, then shake the dust from your feet and move on.

This will be a daily walk as you put distance between yourself and sickness. Don't dwell in the past or worry about the future. Keep your thoughts on this day – today. The day your healing was set in motion. I have included a list of personalized healing scriptures for you to take as medicine. Let My word heal your flesh. If you can 'see' in your mind, the words going into your body and healing you – it is done!

Bless you My child. I will be walking with you every day until it is time for you to return home. But for now, there is more for you to do.

****

Final Words

1. Sunlight is your friend, though not in excess.

2. Fruits, leaves, roots, stems and seeds are for your healing.

3. Avoid toxins, including many medicaments.

4. Surround yourself with supportive people.

5. Set your environment so that you love what you see around you.

6. Guard your mind – forgive others quickly, love unconditionally, and judge no-one.

7. Do not be too hard on yourself. Being kind to yourself isn't selfish, it is necessary.

8. Do not complain.

9. Be grateful for all things, good or bad. (I turn all seemingly bad things around for your good.)

10. Find a 'secret' place where you can bring your burdens to Me in prayer and receive my guidance every day.

11. Enjoy and celebrate each little blessing and success as you heal.

12. Thank Me daily for your health and avoid persons who do not agree that you are healing.

13. No matter what you see or feel, keep speaking health over yourself.

14. Drink plenty of clean water.

15. Rest.

16. Move your body often – Exercise.

17. Spend regular time outdoors in nature.

18. Take communion in memory of My Son. His body and blood bring life and health.

19. Do not depend on other people to make you happy. Happiness comes through the fulfillment of your purpose, and I will be your guide when you seek me in the quiet places.

20. Let go of responsibilities that do not truly belong to you.

21. Let your surroundings be utterly supportive of your health.

******

Healing Scriptures

I have given you a set of words that you may declare over your body. They are your medicine. Take a few minutes up to three times each day to speak them aloud as they become locked into your soul and flesh, and heal your body. You will not have to read every single one every day, as even a few of these will do. Some days you may even select one and digest that one all day. You may repeat them along with the blessing statements from chapter 2 for a complete renewing of your mind. Whatever you do, meditate on them, and let them heal you. You are going to make it. I believe in you! Be thou healed!

****

- o   I will prosper and be in health, even as my soul prospers. (3 John 1: 2)
- o   I will lift my eyes to the hills from whence cometh my help. My help comes from the Lord, who made Heaven and Earth. (Psalm 121:1-2)

- o I am not afraid, because God is with me. I will not be dismayed, because He is my God. (Isaiah 41: 10)
- o My Lord upholds me with His righteous right hand. (Isaiah 41:10)
- o I hope in the Lord, and He is renewing my strength, I will soar on wings like eagles. I will run and not be weary; I will walk and not faint. (Isaiah 40:31)
- o I say to this sickness, Go and throw yourself into the sea, and it will be done for me. (Mark 11:23)
- o This sickness is finished, as it was finished on the cross. (John 19: 30)
- o I curse the root of this sickness; it will dry up like the fig tree and bear no more fruit in my body for ever and ever. (Matthew 21: 18-19)
- o Healing will come to me because I believe it, and it shall be unto me as I believe. (Matthew 8:13)
- o I will not fear for He is with me. (Isaiah 41)
- o I will not be afraid of terror by night, or arrows by day. These will not come near me. (Psalm 91:5)
- o I am covered under God's feathers and under His wings. His truth shall be my shield. (Psalm 91:4)

- The Lord is my refuge and fortress. I will trust Him. (Psalm 91)
- Nothing can separate me from God's love. (Romans 8: 38-39)
- God loves me with an everlasting love. (Jeremiah 31: 3)
- The Lord has plans for me, plans to prosper me and not to harm me, plans to give me hope and a future. (Jeremiah 29:11)
- Jesus took my infirmities and carried sicknesses away from me. I do not have to and will not be sick any longer. (Matthew 8:17)
- I have submitted to God, so now I resist the enemy's sickness and it flees from my body. (James 4:7)
- I remain in God and His words remain in me. I can ask for what I want, and I shall have it. I now ask for and receive good health. (John 15:7)
- The Lord is restoring my health and healing my wounds. (Jeremiah 30:17)
- The Lord has made my inmost parts, knitting me together in my mother's womb. (Psalm 139:13)
- The Lord has forgiven all my sins and healed all my diseases. (Psalm 103:3)

o I am not anxious, but I have prayed with thanksgiving, and have let my requests be known to God, and He has given me peace that surpasses understanding. This peace guards my heart and mind through Christ. (Philippians 4: 6-7)

o I am rejoicing in the Lord. (Philippians 4:4)

o I will only focus on what is noble, right, pure, lovely, admirable, excellent and worthy of praise. (Philippians 4:8)

o The Lord is my light and my salvation, who shall I fear? The Lord is the strength of my life, of whom shall I be afraid? (Psalm 27:1)

o I will lay down and sleep peacefully because my Lord keeps me safe. (Psalm 4:8)

o The Lord is my refuge and strength, a very present help in times of trouble. (Psalm 46:1)

o Even as I walk through the valley of the shadow of death, I will not be afraid. God restores my soul, comforts me, and brings me peace of mind. (Psalm 23)

o I have brought the Lord all my burdens and He has given me rest. (Matthew 11: 28)

- I believe what God says, not what I see. (2 Corinthians 5:7)
- My spirit is cheerful now and this is good medicine. (Proverbs 17:22)
- The Lord has opened my eyes, and now He lifts me up. (Psalm 146:8)
- I will worship the Lord my God, and my food and water is blessed. He has taken sickness from me. (Exodus 23:25)
- Every tear is wiped from my eyes. There is no more death or mourning or crying or pain, for the old order of things has passed away. I am free. (Rev 21:4)
- My heart is trouble-free. I am fearless. (John 14:27)
- The Lord heals all who are sick, and I also am healed. (Mark 6:56)
- I reach out and touch the hem of Jesus' garment and am healed, just like the woman with the issue of blood. (Matthew 9:20-22)
- Because of Jesus' suffering I am healed. (Isaiah 53:4-6)
- Heal me oh Lord and I shall be healed, save me and I shall be saved: for you are my praise. (Jeremiah 17:14)

o The Lord rises over me with healing in his wings. (Malachi 4:2.)

o I will get up, and take up my mat, and go on my way, healed. (Matthew 9: 6-7)

o I reached out and touched the Lord, and His power came out from Him and healed me. (Luke 6: 19)

o Death and life come from what I say, and I will live! (Proverbs 18:21)

o I will receive healing, because I have asked for it, believing that it is my portion. (Matt 21:22)

o My tongue speaks only good things, and I will love and enjoy my life and see good days. (1 Peter 3:10)

o By my faith in God, I can overcome the World. (1 John 5:4-5)

o If the enemy rises against me in one direction, he will be forced to flee from me in seven directions. (Deuteronomy 28:7)

o By not judging others, I avoid judgement myself. I choose to bless others instead. (Matthew 7:1)

o I will have life abundantly because God wants me to. (John 10:10) o I will see the goodness of God in the land of the living. (Psalm 27:13)

o I am blessed because I trust in the Lord. I will be like a tree planted by the water, whose leaves will always be green. (Jeremiah 17:7-8)

o I inherit blessing because I repay evil with blessing by blessing my enemies. (1 Peter 3:9)

o I listen to the Lord; therefore, the Lord heals me. (Exodus 15)

o I have humbled myself and prayed and sought the face of the Lord and turned from my wicked ways, so the Lord will heal me. (2 Chronicles 7:14-15)

o The Lord blesses me and keeps me and makes His face shine upon me, and He is gracious to me. He looks upon me and gives me peace. (Numbers 6:24-26)

o All things are possible because I believe. (Mark 9:23)

******

Dr. Arlene Rose-Lewis is a medical doctor and healing evangelist, wife, and mother of three children. She discovered Jesus after a mind-blowing supernatural experience which was outlined in her first book *Faith medicine and Miracles, a Doctor's Journey into Supernatural Healing*. She has discovered that Jesus still heals and has healed many persons even in these times. She also came to recognize that there are some things that prevented persons from getting well using any method until these were dealt with. In these people, medicine would not work and neither would prayers. She set about to discover these blocking factors and when she did, she began to help people to overcome them. One day during a fast a 'heavenly download' that became this book began. It began with the 'Still Small Voice', speaking quietly as though a lot had to be said that morning. She grabbed a pen and began to scribble by hand every word pouring from God's heart. This continued for almost 10 hours. While she wrote it, she herself learned new things about healing that were opened up before her and explained in new enlightening ways. These writings have forever changed the way she practices medicine, and it is hoped that you too will be forever changed for the better, armed with the information delivered in this book. Dr. Rose-Lewis currently practices dermatology in Kingston, Jamaica.

www.ingramcontent.com/pod-product-compliance
Lightning Source LLC
Chambersburg PA
CBHW061302140726
47998CB00006B/2328